I0843418

WALK TALL WITHIN WALLS

by Karen Kellock Ph.D.

Manual for
Superior Men

A complete theory based on Einstein physics,
Political Psychology, Systems Theory
and Archetypal Psychiatry.

FORMULA

All success attraction
All disease obstruction
All recovery elimination

You must fast on all three

OBSTRUCTIONS:

People
Habit
Food

WALK TALL WITHIN WALLS

Their go-to tactic is spreading rumors about you, making life miserable. They wanna trash your n ame regardless of facts and control how others see you so its death by embarrassment too. A smear campaign is evil, demonic, psychologically abusive and unhealthy but is used mainly. Cut them outa your life once and for all and welcome sanity and eventual lovers of your soul. Home is all, where you walk tall.

IMMATURE GENERATION

THE COLLAPSED NARCISSIST
RAGE TO NOT FACE THEMSELVES
MUST AVOID EVIL BANDS
HE WHO PERSEVERES WINS
PUT THROUGH A MEAT GRINDER
KNOW HOW FAST LIFE CHANGES
LOVEBOMBING AND THEN DOOM
DENIAL OF REALITY
PUTTING INSECURITIES ON YOU
YOU WERE FRESH OIL
WHY SUCCESSFUL PEOPLE HIDE
GOD GIVES YOU WARNING SIGNS
IT'S BETTER TO BE BORED
YOUR HARD WORK PAYS OFF
WHEN LIBERATED FROM MANIPULATION
THE CRUELIST GUARDS STARTED NICE
PTSD AND THE AWFUL MEMORIES

IMMATURE GENERATION

THE COLLAPSED NARCISSIST

Life is a ladder so of course you went thru crap at the bottom but now why must you relive em?

Narcissistic abuse stops only when they die. That may sound harsh but it's the way they are, aye.

The collapsed narcissist goes into extreme isolation. They don't wanna be seen as vulnerable son.

For the collapsed narcissist, attention means bad exposure and they can't take that, ever.

They're like a wild animal cornered and hurt. They'll lash out with the past and it's you they hate first.

RAGE TO NOT FACE THEMSELVES

Rage is an attempt to not face what they've become, a must. Instead they attack and create a fuss.

Any type of narcissist will blame the victim. This is their hallmark so be ready and never give in.

They'll future fake or say "you're the only one" only to bring you down or withdraw the prize hon.

Expect their ruthless blame shifting. They could be on their death bed and it will rear up suddenly.

Get out of their way or pay them off. Get a restraining order as part of the deal if they stay out.

You're fake friends aren't grinding and working like you but feel entitled to your blessings Sue.

IMMATURE GENERATION

I was an extrovert and people-lover but once I saw we're living in the evil days I became an introvert ok.

MUST AVOID EVIL BANDS

People are sticky: it's called evil bands. They're jealous of all you have: must relocate to another land.

You gotta stay out of the way, keep moving, pressing to the HIGH mark which is your own destiny.

You're climbing to a new level: the high calling of Christ Jesus but only by cutting bands so grievous.

People with nothing to lose are dangerous people. If they can't have what's yours they just hate you.

We're not merely afraid of them, we know what the enemy can do. That's real experience Sue.

The enemy comes in three ways: either to kill, steal or destroy. Let them in and gone will be all joy.

We're in spiritual warfare right now. Fake friends & false family contain spirits of destruction, wow.

Once they see you're wise as a serpent & harmless as a dove they get confused: it frustrates em too.

HE WHO PERSEVERES WINS

The battle is not given to the fastest or strongest but he who endures to the end: he's the greatest.

Do you know the jealousy, hatred and envy we must go through to get to the pearly white gates Sue?

Never go to a fight without your secret weapons: that's prayer and resisting the devil [fasting on evil].

IMMATURE GENERATION

Human nonchalance: On the surface it's law and order but behind it is arbitrariness and violence.

As was the case before Nazi Germany, people actions were more of appearance than reality.

The human race is run by fakery: that's the way it's been all through the cycles & devastations in history.

Not just blame the victim for what you've done to them, but doubling down and making hate on them.

Getting others to hate the victim is the essence of social psychology after what you've done to them.

Being put thru this meat grinder changes you forever. It's part of your DNA to isolate or whatever.

"Why do you write of these things" people ask. Cuz it's the human condition all thru the past.

PUT THROUGH A MEAT GRINDER

I was put thru this meat grinder by fake family & friends then researched the holocaust, amen?

The jealous would like nothing better than to take all you have then accuse you/go on the attack.

It's human nature to deflect from self by jumping on the bandwagon & hating a scapegoat, that's all.

The youth live in la-la land of endless optimism. They have not yet learned about crazy humans.

I believe God brings abundance & safety to those who love Him, but only by avoiding evil around em.

I'm wholly optimistic about the future but only by minding my P's & Q's to be biblically sure.

IMMATURE GENERATION

Sin has terrible consequences with the Lord. We're always sinners but the big ones are abhorred.

The main consequence of sin is downed hedges. The evil world flows in & we're totally unprotected.

The Puritans knew this, living totally simple, humble, routinized lives. That's how you end up, aye.

Once my gate is locked I do my duties and take care of my charges. Just do what's next, like farmers.

KNOW HOW FAST LIFE CHANGES

A mature person knows how fast life can change. In an instant catastrophe ruins all you're arranged.

This awareness, or lack of complacency, makes you stick to routines and block all those fiends.

Ordinary, acceptable & "decent" people turned against their Jew neighbors as dangerously evil.

When Nazi propaganda flooded Germany with hatred, mere words became deeds as if sacred.

There's a thing called the "family superself" that will suddenly turn against one/put him thru hell.

Like countries, families & small towns, there are opinion leaders who lead the herd against the one.

I went thru this where nothing I could say or do changed the mind of those hypnotized into this stew.

Most are groupies but the chosen are lone individuals squeezed out of the family or group see.

Due to their noncormity the first half of life is traumatic, the second half healing/trying to get over it.

IMMATURE GENERATION

LOVEBOMBING AND THEN DOOM

There's a lovebombing phase of dictatorships or relationships then it's hell on earth quick.

One thing dictatorships have in common is people don't have time to think. Things happen so fast see.

Things are filled with distractions and building you up to agree like putting you on leave or vacation.

The narcissist will rush you into a decision that brings your life into destruction & bad luck hon'.

If they can't have you no one can and they wanna kill you. Humans are a sick bunch in any milieu.

For all who've felt the great rewards the "begrudging & envious chatter" is all ignored as slander.

You can't talk em out of hating the scapegoat or pitying the victim, their mind is made up, amen.

DENIAL OF REALITY

The counter-chatter just washes off of them. They've heard it all before and that's final friend.

When you start doing better than others that's when they start switching on you: bummers.

Everything was all good when you were a crab at the bottom of the bucket, but now look at it.

You escaped the bucket & they're getting cooked. They wanna bring you back down, the crooked.

When karma is whipping their behind they wanna take everything out on you. Stay hidden Sue!

IMMATURE GENERATION

You can feel it in your gut. There's something up! They're watching as you rise up chump.

PUTTING INSECURITIES ON YOU

They're getting ready to throw all their insecurities on you. Careful, this can go very wrong Sue.

They're not confident & secure enough in their own calling and future for they'll always be losers.

You broke the generational curse so don't hang with those who are stuck down for the worse.

They can't curse what God has blessed. But it's a scary thing when they rise up and get restless.

People are cruel--double cruel--but you only see it when you escape Sue. Now just continue.

The presence of God is all over you so stop mixing your oil with their water or you'll stay a dam fool.

You can't mix oil with water: those people were drowning you and it was a sludgy matter.

YOU WERE FRESH OIL

You were fresh oil that kept the engine running. What happens when you're gone? Disgusting.

Without oil you blow out the engine. Don't hang with dry spirits: they all have bloody bad intentions.

Putting water where oil's supposed to be is hanging with Satan: survival instincts are blocked again.

People with nothing to lose are the most dangerous. You rising up is a clear target of the jealous.

IMMATURE GENERATION

Don't be afraid to say "I shall not die but live." Now those nightmares and unease will lift.

Then I saw why successful people stay out the way. They don't argue but just see them clearly ok.

Successful people take the LONG view. They don't fight it out today but go distant, staying out the way.

I wondered why successful people hide so much. Now I know: it's self-protection from the jealous.

The successful keep HIGH energy always. They do that by staying out the way every minute/all days.

They're gone quick cuz they know the energy around: that someone's watching them, hellbound.

WHY SUCCESSFUL PEOPLE HIDE

The successful ones know they're plotting & plannin' against them so they gotta stay movin'.

Now that God planted my feet on higher ground I'm very grateful but I feel the energy of evil around.

The more you elevate the more their true colors come out. The enemy lashes out feeling the drought.

The enemy is afraid of the man or woman you're becoming: into anyone close he's moving.

Anywhere you go they act weird. Low vibrational zombies with something up their sleeve appear.

When they don't like you they're gonna show you. The devil is bold and they want some of your gold.

Why you think the bible says he's roaming around roaring like a LION? Don't get complacent darlin'.

IMMATURE GENERATION

When they don't like you they tell you straight up. Now they're pretending, to get what you have chump.

Meaning well and doing right by you are two different things. See their actions not their wordings.

God told me I had **EVERYTHING** to lose. So why go back to people who want all that you have too?

GOD GIVES YOU WARNING SIGNS

God told me: how many warning signs must I give you? I felt encroachments day and night, it's true.

They come at you with a haughty, prideful, entitled spirit. Don't say a thing but never forget it.

The days are over going into unknown bars/lounges. It's due to spirits roaming around with grudges.

Pay attention to your surroundings and listen. You gotta be more respectful and beholden to intuition.

You can't even invite people to your house anymore. They carry spirits & they're demonic whores.

The bible says to be ye separate and come out from amongst them **ALL.** Can you do that doll?

God made you chief now, a high position. Don't hang with those who swept you under the rug man.

God made you the head not the tail, so you gotta **STAY** the head not give into encroachers and fail.

IT'S BETTER TO BE BORED

I'd rather be bored with peace of mind than hang with spirits and the confusion they cause, aye.

IMMATURE GENERATION

When you have to fight for privacy it's time to put on the whole armor of God, that's all I gotta say.

Stay away from people with nothing to lose and the fiery darts of Satan which come with em too.

God chose you to have your OWN. It's YOU who is blessed not those clowns roaming around.

YOUR HARD WORK PAYS OFF

Hard work pays off. They haven't been grinding all day and night like you with faith in goals far off.

You're anointed: blessed & highly favored. They're ready to take it all out on you, God's peculiar.

Don't rush the process in setting your own business, til you learn how to deal with these spirits.

Slow success builds character and fast success builds ego. Stay in your own lain, easy and slow.

Protect your energy at all cost and stay out of people's face. This isn't the time to pick fights ok.

You have the MEDICINE: your energy is medicine to people's souls and must be protected friend.

They need your divine energy to get to their next level. But then they screw up, back in with the devil.

They have the wrong kind of energy or spirit which pulls you down all the way to the ground: know it.

WHEN LIBERATED FROM MANIPULATION

When liberated from human manipulation you see the stars and moon for the first time: elation!

IMMATURE GENERATION

The wicked bands of humans are an evil cobweb eclipsing your soul until you've made gold.

After going thru the likes of that you never allow control again. No matter what you stay free, amen.

Never allow em in your house, stay free of lush and louse. You keep to your own/love your spouse.

THE CRUELIST GUARDS STARTED NICE

The cruelest prison guards began as the nicest people you ever met. They loved their dog and cat.

If blessed by God they're gonna come around with hands held out. Relocate & find a new route.

Man has two sides nice & cruel and if you have more than them the other shows thru real soon.

A fool is easily separated from his money so can God finally trust you to be a good steward honey?

I hate to be so blunt about this but you're lookin' at one who was thrice taken to the cleaners sis.

I wasn't brought up in the hood but feel like I was by not listening to my parents in childhood.

The WWII camp survivor said "if I talk about it I can't keep living see, the memories will kill me"

PTSD AND THE AWFUL MEMORIES

That's the way PTSD is see. You can talk it out but it never leaves if you feed these awful memories.

They don't know anything, they were never taught because Mom was drunk and Dad was gone.

IMMATURE GENERATION

It's embarrassing curbing an elder about boundaries when they shoulda been taught as kiddies.

In an adulterous generation it's utter chaos. There may be a veil of "I love you" til it turns to a mess.

How easily love turns to pure torture. When jealousy is triggered or when ego is pushed to the rear.

True commitment and lasting love is of mature men but with others childhood trauma crashes in.

"It takes a lifetime to get over those experiences from the camps" and usually it never happens, alas.

It's sad we're defined by these memories but maybe it's a good thing if it gives us solid boundaries.

"I was invaded, tortured and put down as manure" but it takes what it takes to make us mature.

TRIBULATIONS OF THE CHOSEN

THE SHOCK OF BETRAYAL
GENIUS GOES UNNOTICED
THE IRONY OF DESTROYERS
THEY'RE UNAWARE OF YOUR CRIES
STILL STANDING AFTER ALL THAT
THE WAR RESHAPED YOU WELL
BEWARE OF EVIL HELPERS
IT ALL COMES DOWN TO ENVY
ENVY SPIRALS INTO RUIN
YOU WERE PROOF OF POTENTIAL
THE TRIALS ARE FOR PREPARATION
HOW MOSES WAS PREPARED: TRIALS
THEY ACT LIKE YOU DON'T EXIST
YOU MADE MISTAKES AS A CHILD
THE WELL-KNOWN UNKNOWN
EASY TO PREY ON?

TRIBULATIONS OF THE CHOSEN

THE SHOCK OF BETRAYAL

Treachery & betrayal so shocked me I became calm from then on. Every act deliberate with aplomb.

The life of chosens is marked by unimaginable trials that feel surreal. Betrayals mostly & humiliations too.

Unthinkable cruelty followed at every turn. It was deliberate to crush something extraordinary sir.

Every tear and scheme was meant to erase you before the world could witness your brilliance see.

The brightest stars are forged in the deepest darkness. Hunted like an animal, becoming the mostess.

You were ridiculed and rejected only to become a great scientific discoverer or artistic pathbreaker.

Greats were banished & publicly humiliated only to discover things that changed humanity forever.

GENIUS GOES UNNOTICED

Van Gogh's genius went unnoticed in life but his name now echoes thru the ages, that's no lie.

The journeys of genius began with torment, rejection and pain. Every one of them, I'll say it again.

Those struggles were the furnace refining greatness. Your wounds are not your end your highness.

Your wounds are the birth of your story's unstoppable power so don't let em make you sour.

TRIBULATIONS OF THE CHOSEN

What was done to you was brutal, deliberate and a sickness beyond belief--by friends/family see?

They sensed the seed of greatness and wanted you erased before you discovered your case.

Against all odds here you stand, bruised but undefeated. You're high on life tho' cheated.

You were broken in places but with a strength that defies explanation: bold/humble yet defiant.

THE IRONY OF DESTROYERS

The irony: in their twisted efforts to destroy you they gave you what they feared most: genius too.

What you endured wasn't for nothing. What was done to you will make you famous, chosen darlings!

You will be grateful to God for all your tribulations once you see the wonderful, awe-inspiring outcomes.

Being chosen is a paradox & riddle few can comprehend: not just fame, fortune and glory friend.

It's far from a path paved with endless blessings. It's not a path of ease but struggle, hatred & lynchings.

It is isolation and pain that few can understand. Being chosen is public humiliation   and   opprobrium.

Those who admire you for your success are blind to the dark shadows that led you here, the distress.

THEY'RE UNAWARE OF YOUR CRIES

They're unaware of nights you cried yourself to sleep, when betrayal made you question all you see.

TRIBULATIONS OF THE CHOSEN

They don't know about the years your doubted your worth, when you felt like a mere grasshopper.

Being chosen is about the journey that broke and rebuilt you. The smashing of the old self to build anew.

It's about surviving in a world which seems to crush you. It's about a sick stomach from felt evil too.

It's not about strongest or gifted but emerging whole from the unimaginable wreckage of old.

STILL STANDING AFTER ALL THAT

Still standing and holding onto hope. That's how God sees you, His peculiar darling: pure gold.

Why did you have to endure so much, so uniquely personal trials? Think of Job in the Bible.

Job was chosen not cuz he was great but for enduring unimaginable suffering and still praise.

Trials were not random but a greater plan. Endurance brought rewards greater than his losses then.

Our road is lonely but deeply purposeful. Look at it that way and you won't feel distressed but fulfilled.

The most devastating wars are fought in silence where no one else can see the inner turbulence.

It was a covert war raged against your mind, spirit and very sense of self. Still you held on thru hell.

THE WAR RESHAPED YOU WELL

The war was so deep it reshaped every part of who you are. You're. an entirely different person now.

TRIBULATIONS OF THE CHOSEN

Envy is a quiet corrosive force, hidden behind smiles. They made you feel small because of it, aye.

Envy is a sickness pushing people to destroy what they can't have nor become. You faced that son.

Evil never reveals itself directly. It wears many disguises and it destroys by getting in your good graces.

BEWARE OF EVIL HELPERS

Criticism, sabotage or the false cloak of "help". Evil helpers brought me down the most, watch out.

How they do it: by telling you your dreams are unrealistic. Of course those bums couldn't see it.

These words weren't from truth, but their inability to stand seeing you rise and take charge Sue.

Your. success reminds them of their own shortcomings and insecurities, that's how it is certainly.

How many times I faced that subtle attack: that I was dreaming too big or too high so accept lack.

Their words are reflections of their painful inner turmoil and inescapable need to pull you down.

Their need is to make you doubt yourself and dim your light. Oh, that light! That's what it is guys.

IT ALL COMES DOWN TO ENVY

They wanna feel comfortable in their shadows. For a while it worked as you questioned your worth.

You tried to SHRINK yourself or fit their molds to dampen their discomfort, but hardly triumphant.

TRIBULATIONS OF THE CHOSEN

You may have felt guilty for standing out or not meeting their expectations. This too is defeating son.

Envy destroys the carrier far more than the target. It's why they seem so empty, don't you know it?

You were never their competition but a living example of what was possible, but it broke em down so.

Your success was a reminder of what they never dared believe for themselves--you were the magic elf.

Cain's inability to rule over his jealousy led him to tragic decision. Conquer it or the result is ruin.

ENVY SPIRALS INTO RUIN

Envy will spiral into ruin if not addressed. King Saul's envy of David's popularity led to a huge mess.

Despite David's innocence, Saul couldn't bare the thought of someone else rising to prominence.

Saul's envy blinded him to David's integrity/God's plan. His obsession with David's success destroyed him.

In the envy, the very envy that tried to break you will consume them. It's even happening now friend.

They will never understand that you were never their rival. There's no competition between good and evil.

If they had only believed in themselves see, you were a testament to the heights they could reach.

YOU WERE PROOF OF POTENTIAL

You were proof of what could happen if one dares to believe, but that's something they could never see.

TRIBULATIONS OF THE CHOSEN

A heart at peace gives life to the body but envy rots the bones. That's how it turns back on em all.

The trials transforming you into a diamond were hard, brutal and seeming entirely unjust. That's how it was.

The universe doesn't test worthiness with kindness, but stripping you down to bare nothingness.

The "test" stripped you down to the pure essence of who you are: the quintessential is the star.

THE TRIALS ARE FOR PREPARATION

The trials which keep coming are not meant to punish you but prepare you. They seem unfair too.

Greatness demands great strength. That's what you have after suffering people problems in effect.

The suffering you endured was a fire burning away the superficial layers: the raw unfiltered mires.

When everything you relied on is stripped away, who are you? What do you stand for, do you know Sue?

How do you respond when 10,000 are against you? This is the test of the greatest amongst us too.

Job was so tested that all he had left was his faith. This is the end run, the test of the greatest I say.

HOW MOSES WAS PREPARED: TRIALS

Before Moses took on the monumental role of leading out of Egypt he had to endure much hardship.

His years in the wilderness were not punishment but preparation. I did that, living in a tiny cabin.

TRIBULATIONS OF THE CHOSEN

God is preparing the bruised chosen for the immense responsibility ahead, to be fully/faithfully led.

Moses stepped into his divine purpose made impossible had he not been shaped by those very trials.

Could it be your struggles are preparing you for something greater than you can ever imagine?

No one asks for hardship that seem to break their spirit. But the outcome is what you've always wanted.

You were chosen for ability to rise above chaos that would break most others: you really suffered.

Not everyone survives these tests. Most get caught in the pain, unable to let it go and live again.

But you're still here, still standing. You made it and shine like a diamond, prepared and ready.

THEY ACT LIKE YOU DON'T EXIST

They act like you don't exist but energy never lies: they KNOW you're one of God's chosen in disguise.

They act like you're not doing anything but you are: it's God's work and it's day energy you're fulfilling.

If they can't celebrate you, never go in their presence again. For the chosen that's how it is friend.

They cry at your funeral but where were they when you were hurting and going thru that struggle?

They will travel miles and miles when you're dead but act like you don't exist when a success.

When you are chosen by God you have energy that makes them hate you. This explains it Sue.

TRIBULATIONS OF THE CHOSEN

Do you feel celebrated when you walk in? Do you feel congratulated walking into the door friend?

You think I'm lying? Keep living and keep winning. Things are exposed about human beings.

They counted you out. They left you for dead. When you walked up they always said "you again?"

YOU MADE MISTAKES AS A CHILD

They knew who you were as a child when you made mistakes and fell on your face, disgraced.

The new you says "I know you gave up on me and threw me to the wolves but I still love you sis".

God has been so good to you, you don't ever stoop to their level of manipulation and destruction.

The reason you've been picked on is cuz by God you've been picked out. From birth, it's how it was.

God handpicked you out of your group of friends and your family. That's why spirits target thee.

You're the light surrounded by darkness so of course there will be repercussions with all of this.

THE WELL-KNOWN UNKNOWN

They act like you don't exist but are always spying online to see your accomplishments.

They act like you don't exist but are fascinated by your every move or are present at your funeral.

They won't look you in the eye or act like you're in the room yet seek to know all about you too.

TRIBULATIONS OF THE CHOSEN

The chosen feels like the most ignored person on earth yet everyone knows all about him since birth.

You feel he disdains you even hates your guts but actually he loves you: that's the whats.

They MUST ignore you for you've been chosen, not them. But your light is still evident friend.

He feels invisible, yet is the well-known unknown since all know his darkest secrets from gossip.

EASY TO PREY ON?

They thought you were easy to prey on only to witness you were ten steps ahead and then GONE.

The bible says be not ignorant concerning Satan and his devices. God doesn't want us used & despised.

That's why we're the PRAY before our next move. Looking on all sides, finding the right groove.

Keep your grass low so the Lord will keep revealing these snakes. Stay sober, alert & awake!

I was surrounded by those thinking I was naive and gullible. Then karma hit and they went to hell.

One way of keeping your grass low is to avoid all chaos and streamline all routines. Simplicity is keen.

They ALL took your kindness for weakness so the result is a big deal: stay alert now or they'll steal.

They use you as an ATM machine, ongoing withdrawals outa your life. Thinking nothing of asking, aye.

What deposits have they made into your life? They have deceived you for your money honey, aye.

TRIBULATIONS OF THE CHOSEN

You were judging by appearances/sleeping with the enemy but now you see they deceived you honey.

The whole world is besmirched by wolves in sheep's clothing. That accounts for evil in everything.

Most people are manipulators. And they get big mad when they don't get their way: careful sister.

PERSECUTION AND REJECTION

PERECUTION WAS NECESSARY
BOLD AND STRONG FROM OVERCOMING
NEW PEOPLE WILL LOVE YOU
NOW RESCUED, DON'T LOOK BACK
GOD CREATED YOU TO SHINE
DEALING WITH REJECTION
YOU'VE FELT THIS BEFORE
THO' IT HURTS, TURN IT AROUND
REJECTORS CAN'T SEE YOU

PERSECUTION AND REJECTION

You're a brave one who handles situations with class and dignity, but it was a rough road see.

Intelligence, radiance and dignity is your reward for coming through this humiliating war.

Recognize the persecution was necessary for you to flourish and walk in your purpose/destiny.

As painful as it was it was necessary to get you to the next level, so get past painful PTSD pal.

I had PTSD so bad I was pissed off all the time. That's no way to reach success written in the sky.

I don't know who was worse, the men or the Jezebel women tormenting me when I was down.

PERECUTION WAS NECESSARY

It was necessary so persecutors had right thoughts towards you & to feel God's revenge too.

Coals of ashes on their head: it's God's promise it would turn around with them down instead.

The truth is: men or women for God's heavenly kingdom would face a lot in this life, even bedlam.

God said your walk wouldn't be easy and you realize that now. But the rewards are great: wow!

People are gonna despise you, mock you and hate you. It is a promise so don't be surprised Sue.

How you feel about yourself in this process trumps it all. Knowing what will happen blunts your fall.

PERSECUTION AND REJECTION

The group hurt me so much I had a sour gut constantly as their social hypnotism kicked my butt.

On the way up they're your friend but going down they can't wait to join in your fall/create bedlam.

It's the Fallen Hero Syndrome: it teaches you about people & their duplicity even in your home.

This persecution had to happen so you could finally stand out. It took that my friend so don't pout.

BOLD AND STRONG FROM OVERCOMING

You're so bold and strong now from what you went thru. It's written in your DNA now, on your face too.

Those who've rejected/humiliated you have come to nothing while you're a bright light darling.

God did not call you to wallow in the background so timid as you were, He wants you a STAR.

They humiliated and talked against you, not wanting to see your beauty, divinity and goodness too.

They only wanted to point out your flaws and they did that constantly to anyone and all.

But your holy God above accepted you and your flaws, seeing who you WOULD be after it all.

NEW PEOPLE WILL LOVE YOU

God will line you up with those who accept you despite your flaws, even see them as cute [ah].

New people won't embarrass and humiliated you every chance they get like "family & friends" did.

PERSECUTION AND REJECTION

It's like they loved to hate & despise you. They even said it to your face when you had no defense too.

You were meant to stand out at this time so don't worry about these people anymore, it's all divine.

As these old networks disperse like a vapor, you meet a new life with energy and even glamour.

Those that lied on your name in the worst way possible will now face God's revenge on the evil.

Your persecutors were filled with flaws but wouldn't accept yours. Hypocrisy that runs this war.

NOW RESCUED, DON'T LOOK BACK

God removed & rescued you saying "don't look back or go back again" as they dispersed in the wind.

They chose not to see your value and loved putting you down to anyone who would listen too.

When it came to you their eyes were blind but you my friend will just continue to grow & shine.

Now you can be the star that you are. It's all from successfully coming thru this biblical war.

The Psalms says it: Kings of the earth gather together to bring God's men down and laugh about it.

They persecuted you like they did Yeshua on the cross. Couldn't see your light and called you lost.

They hated on you cuz that's what they love to do. It's the human race and Satan's influence too.

GOD CREATED YOU TO SHINE

PERSECUTION AND REJECTION

God created you to shine bright in FRONT of your critics and naysayers. They'll all see it for sure.

You are wonderfully and beautifully made in God's image. He said it so believe it: you're a sage.

Those who didn't accept you at your best don't deserve to be around so throw em out of your nest.

At your lowest moments they kicked you lower. Even your own sister or brother made you cower.

It no longer matters who's on your side or isn't. God made you to stand alone not with peasants.

My heart is not proud, my eyes are not haughty. But Lord my foes were, behold the ungodly!

Don't look at the past cuz a saint sees only his glaring mistakes. The others couldn't care less ok.

You are a true leader and don't need to follow anyone. You're too codependent: just be alone.

You were never meant to take a backseat to someone else. You're meant to stand out not feel less.

The persecution was necessary so you wouldn't get comfortable around those people see.

DEALING WITH REJECTION

Don't be hurt rejected and mocked for He called you for greater--so stand straight and suck it up.

Someone meant to be a leader of group or city shouldn't be hurt when rejected by some lady.

Sure it hurts but buck up. Recall you've been through this before and it never helps to suck up.

PERSECUTION AND REJECTION

You did everything to make it better and they only got colder. It's a funny thing about people sir.

Let them go and be alone for awhile. Gather your forces and pray to God who never rejects with guile.

The duplicity of people is shocking. Like a flipped switch their heart turns off and your rocking.

Don't try to get em back, that's not the way. Get YOU back cuz you never felt loved by em anyway.

Don't start drinking/drugging cuz that only degrades. Now's the time to be pure then you'll be ok.

Don't fight back, argue or plead. Silence is the only answer in these times of changed levels see.

New level, new devil: become alert. This is very serious because suddenly you feel so insecure.

YOU'VE FELT THIS BEFORE

You've been thru this before, starting in junior high. It's the panicky feeling of lost dependency, aye.

I've been thru this too, it's a feeling in the gut. That's the solar plexus detecting the same old rut.

Don't play games cuz that makes you too involved with them. Just come inside to you & God friend.

You were supposed to stand out, not settle for less than you deserve. That's why this happened sir.

Accept rejection as a good thing. I know it doesn't feel that way now but God has other plans see.

Things weren't right with that relationship. You made it right so this rift was necessary to reveal it.

PERSECUTION AND REJECTION

You walked on eggs and palliated things for so long it's a shock when the obvious reveals the wrong.

Your gut, the solar plexus, senses a change in the environment. I know it hurts but listen to it.

This is your moment to shine and radiate. So stay pure and anticipate your next adventure ok?

If your gut hurts I'd go into a fast. This puts you in a higher reality so you can even have a blast.

THO' IT HURTS, TURN IT AROUND

Tho' this hurts, turn it all around. See it as a good thing and buck up I'm telling you, you're profound.

Have the enlightenment that they were never meant for you anyway. You knew this but accepted reality.

All changes are a shock to the system. That's what ages us quickly so don't let it be: pray to God man.

Let rejectors fade in your mind. Don't let em seem bigger as his turnoff seems to make him shine.

This is your moment to grow. Sad events like this have great power if you use them right, I know.

Don't look for human support for you never had it before. It was all a waste of time, for sure.

You never had any support to begin with so why look for it now. Fast, pray and then you'll say: WOW!

God says "don't worry about them, I am your biggest support". Protect your emotions like a fort.

God is helping you to get where He wants you to go. Tho' it hurts so much He is doing this now.

PERSECUTION AND REJECTION

You were like a Joseph in your family. Despised by your siblings you got used to those feelings see.

Construct a wall around yourself. Pull in your emotions and bring out your talents, be the magic elf.

Their love was flaky. It was "I love you" robotically but then like a switch it all turned cold see.

When trust is gone, how can we feel that love again darlin'? True enduring love is rarely found.

His love is gone, the gleam is gone from his eyes. So forget him where he's at & don't even try.

When it happened to me I would beg and plead. When it comes to love this will make it worse see.

You got so tired of his words of love all day long. You knew it was robotic, so what if its "gone".

REJECTORS CAN'T SEE YOU

A rejector can't see the star, the bright light that you are. That's not something you want back, no sir.

Why does he only miss you when you're gone? You don't want that back, you must move on.

All the hell and chaos she caused but she "misses you" when you're gone. It doesn't make sense son.

Don't take the blame and rest now. For you truly are the man or woman God called you to be, wow.

Your Father in heaven doesn't want you to feel like this. Buck up now, go forward/fast into His bliss.

You can be a peace from this matter now, not later. An event changed his heart but God is your Father.

PERSECUTION AND REJECTION

Let God protect you from this pain you had no control over. Rest in him from Joseph's brothers.

God knew what they'd do to you before you were born. This is an archetype you would overcome.

Cast yourself out to the sea of forgiveness and forget em all. Hole in cuz this was a serious fall.

Now you can be an inspiration to others who are being rejected and scorned. Buck up, and go on.

WALK TALL WITHIN WALLS

RAISE YOUR DISGUST LEVEL
DISGUST SAVES THE HOME
ARROGANT ENTITLED KIDS
FEMINISTS JUSTIFY EVIL
LIBERAL LUNACY
THEY SEE ONLY RACISM EVERYWHERE
BORN FOR SUCH A TIME AS THIS
ENVY MAKES EM CRUEL AND BITTER
INSTIGATORS
BACKFIRE OF NARCISSIST TACTICS
TALK OR COUGH: BODY MIND INTEGRATION
SPEAK TO RECOVER FROM TRAUMA
HOSTILE ENVIRONMENTS ARE HELLISH
YOUR EMOTIONS & TRUTH ARE VALID!
IT HURTS TO BE MISJUDGED
DESPERATE DESIRE FOR LOVE FILLING
THE HERO'S PATH IS CIRCUITOUS
EMPTY TRADITION ROBS SELF-ESTEEM
NEIGHBORHOOD MISPERCEPTIONS
IF THEY COME WITH AN ARMY [FLYING MONKEYS]
DATING PROCESS VETS THE DROSS
IF HE HATES YOUR SUCCESS WITHDRAW MISS
AMERICANS WERE DECENT: THINK OF THE ANIMALS!
RICH LEFTIST SNOBS ENJOY WALLS
BRINGING IN THE *HORRIBLY* BACKWARDS
GLOBALISTS HATE FREE ECONOMIES
STATE'S RIGHTS MEANS ANTI-GLOBALIST
DUMPING ILLEGALS FOR FREE VACATIONS
VICTORY WAS THROUGH TERROR

WALK TALL WITHIN WALLS

POLITICAL CORRECTNESS FOR SAKE OF ISLAM
GREEN IS THE NEW RED
SPEEDBUMPS AND DETRACTORS
LOVING TRUMP IS THE LITMUST TEST
TRUMP'S TURNED PROSPERITY BACK ON
NFL WERE GLOBALIST TOOLS YOU FOOLS
NATIONALISM IS NOT RACISM
ELITES PUT BLINDERS AND GAGS ON AMERICANS
INTENSE NATIONALISM FROM SUDDEN REVELATIONS
THEY WANT US RENTERS FOR CONTROL
"STARS" MEANS SATAN'S IN THERE
PRAY FOR THE SPIRIT OF JUSTICE
LIBERTY *ALWAYS* TRUMPS TYRANNY
GLOBALIST WORLD ENGINEERS
GLOBALISTS HIJACKED OUR COUNTRY
THE CIA RUNS THE "WOMEN'S MARCHES"
LEFT: POWER FROM RHETORIC AND RIOTS
MEXICO IS CARTELS AND TORTURE
TRUMP TOOK OUR NATION BACK
GLOBALISTS IN DEATH THROES
THEY ACTUALLY HATE PROSPERITY
THEIR PSYCHOLOGY: BRING DOWN THE WEST
ARROGANT CREEPS PAID BY GLOBALIST SCUM
PULL THE PLUG, TURN OFF THE SPIGOT!
GLOBALISTS CONSOLIDATE NO MATTER WHAT
THE SOROS JUDGES
ELITES WANT NEO-FEUDALISM AGAIN
PANACEA: DELETE ALL RAINBOW FRIENDS
HEALTHY UPDATES AND YOUTUBE MATES

WALK TALL WITHIN WALLS

"I can't get back at them cuz most are dead so I had to write all these books instead" Karen said.

How wonderful life is when it's just me. Having to adapt to their squabbles & dramas wss torture see.

Parents loved me the most at first but sisters talked them outa that fast. Like prodigal son, jealous.

The torture of control by human nature pierced the mystic center and out came divine nectar.

Ignore all the time that has passed my friend. I'm gonna make it big it's just a matter of when.

When you conger the bloody past, think: that was another era of schooling, a different life see.

I was bad but what came first the chicken or egg? I was stressed, needed solace from being pegged.

With PTSD the war is never over. It's the jungle mentality of shooting at shadows/running for cover.

RAISE YOUR DISGUST LEVEL

He has no ordering skills: the junkman. He seems lost and hopeless without me but I love him.

The disorderly junkman is a work in progress, that's what I keep sayin' so I'll follow him around.

I'll pick up his socks if he just pays the dam bills! Look at it like that: just keep order and be still.

WALK TALL WITHIN WALLS

I'm half German and I want things neat and orderly. Every culture's different in this tendency.

I'm half Scotch and want solitude and privacy. Announce yourself always or you're an enemy.

The height of your boundary reflects level of disgust for the enemy--those you haven't vetted see.

You don't just trust anyone if Scotch. It's wait and see, not like the new age loving everyone so much.

It's not give em the benefit of the doubt if not knowing the alien but loyalty proven with time, amen.

DISGUST SAVES THE HOME

The height of my wall reflects my disgust level and that is a good thing for home, quite wonderful.

As a child I had no disgust level, not knowing anything at all. But maturity looks different at y'all.

Just be disgusted but don't show it. You don't have to be haughty about it but notice the difference.

The new age threw us out there to accept everything as one. That was pure destruction/false fun.

You should want your independent life sequestered from the others. Not conformity, that smothers.

They wanted me to conform to such low level bullshevik it literally made me sick like other lunatics.

Innate genius will never come out if needing approval. Can't fit square into a circle/be above it all.

I could never figure out what to do to gain approval anyway, it was such a weird world ok.

WALK TALL WITHIN WALLS

I felt homesick in kindergarten--for the dysfunctional family, that's how trauma works friend.

And when the highschoolers of '85 invaded me I felt the same way times a thousand: hell to pay.

ARROGANT ENTITLED KIDS

They were imposing, invasive, disorderly, boundary busting, thieving, time wasting frenemies.

The boomers were bad but how do they stand their kids let alone their grand kids in this era Dad?

And if you got good herb and they don't have any they'll bust down your doors honey, I know see.

I got herb to last one year and they wanted to consume it in a night, that's one example of the fight.

Because their feminist moms refused to punish, predictably the brats ended in prison, felons.

FEMINISTS JUSTIFY EVIL

It wasn't so much THEM as it was what feminism does to women. They're a herd, a clique echoin'.

With those two girls my identity was always on the line. A hypersensitive throwing pearls before swine.

The feminist moms always justify kids badness from childhood problems and that's the result sis.

Children reflect moods of their mother: if she's a drunken belligerent scrapper they copy her.

He hated Trump so I unsubbed the psychiatrist. If he thinks like that I want nothing from the twit.

WALK TALL WITHIN WALLS

If you're not anti-white you're a racist. Notice how the overton window has shifted: new matrix.

Our leaders went from rich suburb to elite college to a DC think tank/lobbyist: not the wisest.

I went from a rich suburb to the desert wilderness in a cabin to learn everything about life sis.

U.S. military says diversity and inclusion are necessities and that means we're toast, dead, history.

LIBERAL LUNACY

Liberal lunacy: Not arresting criminals is "taking a principled stand against white supremacy".

The bottom of society relished in the moment of our beautiful cities being burned down, truly.

These people won't stop until we all look like Tijuana. We must now get out the vote for America.

"The family" was a feeling of being railroaded and mobbed by a buncha self-righteous slobs.

Without gossiping women have nothing. Don't you know that's how they rule their domain?

Reverse anti-white racism is pushed by handsomely paid "diversity consultants", how arrogant.

THEY SEE ONLY RACISM EVERYWHERE

They say racism is everywhere in the schools see: even math, grammar, spelling and geography.

They're drilling shame and remorse into children about what happened before they were born.

WALK TALL WITHIN WALLS

They prioritized woke initiatives loved by a small bicoastal minority and ignored flyover country.

Fentanyl is 50 times more deadly than heroin and most death <45 is from that stats are showin'

The democrat policy is to get as many illegals here as possible so they don't care about fentanyl.

All fentanyl comes across the southern border so they can't say they care if they don't closer her.

They can spend limitless cash on anything they want but one new border patrol agent? NOT.

Liberals talk so much about slavery but not the holocaust far more gross and racist.

Trudeau accepted that deal on top of the mountain and now he's under their control for millennium.

As bad as it was slavery's not as bad as the holocaust with millions of bodies piled up.

Liberals never discuss {or they deny} holocaust: since the RACIAL victims were white, no loss.

I lived in fear of what they'd say about me next. Liberals accuse you of what they do/I was stressed.

People are lost, don't know what to do so they channel their innate hate to the unvaccinated ok.

In Canada there's been no love connection just demoralization but now it's here AMEN!

BORN FOR SUCH A TIME AS THIS

I was born for such a time as this. After the war, facing and writing of the same human prejudice.

WALK TALL WITHIN WALLS

They didn't hate me for being black, brown or jewish. They hated me for being different: newish.

Hate is hate and if feeling squeezed out study the holocaust to see what humans are all about.

It wasn't just the Germans acting that way, the Japs did too. All have two sides but different levels.

Study the holocaust and their bashings won't hurt so much. It's universal and historical as such.

People just wanna feel superior: uppity vis-a-vis a target. The bible calls it haughty/stiffnecked.

The more unique, different, new and groundbreaking you are the more hate comes near and far.

It's hard dealing with hate so we tend to fall into our bag of devices to cope then this brings blame.

Facing hate without addictive device is making gold and evolving high like historical personages, aye.

ENVY MAKES EM CRUEL AND BITTER

Envy makes em cruel and bitter. They age fast from this crap but you my friend are SO much better.

After your holocaust get a face lift, go on a diet--anything you gotta do to start a new life.

Abuse are usually in denial about the extent of what's been done to them so victims see it now.

The worst possible memory is them abusing or taking your pet. It's how they fight so get a fence.

If adversity only bend a man it just makes him better. The worse it was the more you evolve higher.

WALK TALL WITHIN WALLS

Shame and remorse: Always recall the **BEST** saints were the **WORST** sinners. Now forget it sir.

After being degraded and ignored for years by Trudeau the truckers are now high on love and hope.

The extreme prejudice of two sisters against one feels like same prejudice in Nazi Germany hon'.

A matter of degree. They can't put you in a concentration camp but make your life very sad.

I lost penthouse and jaguaar but God doubled His exemplar and now I own a whole town/2 cars.

Double for your trouble--that's a promise of the bible and It's true folks, I'm so grateful and humble.

They would prop up my enemies, any foe of mine was automatically their friend: that is treachery.

INSTIGATORS

I could never tell them about a new job or beau cuz they'd run behind and ruin it all: how pitiful.

God took me outa the whole mess, I outlived my enemies and am surrounded by love/gaiety.

It coulda just been they had blue eyes and mine were brown. It's possible, knowing what I know.

Nazism didn't stop with the war. Some blond females hated their own sister cuz she was dark.

Now it's changed and they hate ya cuz you're white. Hate is everywhere always so accept it, aye.

Their go-to covert tactic is always to spread rumors about you, making life painfully miserable.

WALK TALL WITHIN WALLS

They wanna trash your name regardless of facts. See what they did to Trump: that's how it is.

Cinderella Syndrome isn't just a myth and tale it's reality in the human drama and scary as hell.

She will control how others see/view you especially after no longer in contact, that's her rule.

She's gonna control how others think about you and thus its death by embarrassment too.

They love stirring the pot being instigators--that's how they get narcissistic supply of course.

Their goal is to get more people on board with them against you and the narc's army is cruel.

A smear campaign is evil, demonic, psychologically abusive and unhealthy but is used mainly.

Cut them outa your life once and for all and welcome sanity and eventual lovers of your soul.

BACKFIRE OF NARC TACTICS

Toxic members are always working in secret to bring the scapegoat down-- secrecy is all they know.

As long as they went along with this they are flying monkeys and just as much to blame.

Block them all, none will change. They got too much outa this hate, discard and smear campaign.

Especially as you get up into your later years, don't waste one more minute on these haters.

Haters gonna hate, haters wanna hate, that's what they do all day, you were just a target ok.

WALK TALL WITHIN WALLS

There's always backlash. Look how arrogantly Nazis invaded the east then froze, trashed.

Demons are arrogant at first, that's how it works. Don't worry, they'll be mowed down in due course.

Their faces are like Martians: the conquerors. Steel flint/self-confident but then they're goners.

Despite all they did and no matter how much evidence they will deny their actions to the end.

As the narcissist ages his abuse tactics will get more intense, his delusions more ridiculous.

TALK OR COUGH: BODY MIND INTEGRATION

Cellular memory: Your body keeps the score of all the abuse even though you can't remember it.

NOT expressing yourself can lockup in throat diseases. That's an example of what happens see.

It is reverse trauma turned into throat diseases: the doctors never ask "were you silenced?"

When I stopped talking I started coughing. Talk or cough: the body mind integration is obvious.

The serious pain trauma from abusive sisters and momma didn't even abate with marijuana.

The therapy is to speak the truth: even if toxic siblings and retaliatory narc don't like it, do it.

As a child I knew I couldn't speak the truth cuz silence was surviving and not being attacked too.

One doctor took my side with abusive sister. I stuck to him like glue then I broke out further.

WALK TALL WITHIN WALLS

Once you're muted and they have attorneys they feel they can do anything and get off free.

If you got sick after decades of being silenced then part of your healing is speaking about this.

Standing up for yourself/speaking the truth about abuse is associated with healing the body too.

SPEAK TO RECOVER FROM TRAUMA

Having courage to tell your story even to one person will show an upswing in your health friend.

When your sister is a pathological liar and your reputation is on fire call on your heavenly Father.

Limit your confidences to only those who are trauma-informed. It's serious but you are normal.

As you approach the end allow yourself to FADE from the world while getting closer to Lord.

One holy doctor saw my plight [with abusive older sisters with lawyers] so I could safely recover.

No-contact means you don't speak to these people again. Demons, thieves, not your friends.

So what if the perpetrators are dead--their flying monkeys aren't and they're just as bad.

Your nephews & nieces seeming so innocent were just as complicit as they did nothing to stop it.

You can't blame monkeys for the narc but you can hold them accountable for helping the sharks.

Trauma is not just trapped in our brain but in every cell and DNA, that's why you feel that way.

WALK TALL WITHIN WALLS

HOSTILE ENVIRONMENTS ARE HELLISH

I had the innate feeling there was nothing my sister wouldn't do especially being stupid too.

You can walk away from an unstable friend but a crazy sister [who's in control] is hell below.

Individuation and maturity is disentrenching old systems keeping you down [status quo it's called].

They hate you with a seething inescapable hatred and there's nothing you can ever do about it.

But when there's two of em--two sister haters arm in arm--your life is over, it's all triangulation.

After I finally escaped the system the one sister became a communist called "progressive".

I don't have to see you just cuz you wanna see me. Where were you before phony frenemy?

After being silenced for decades I'm finally talking and my physical health is reviving & thriving.

Block just about everyone. If you don't trust her completely, get rid of Jezebel a frenemy.

If there's one little thing you hold back from telling her, get rid of this frenemy right now girl.

YOUR EMOTIONS & TRUTH ARE VALID!

Sibling abuse is more likely to be criminal since it's all hidden and the victim has been silenced.

Incest, molestation, pimping out your sister to your friends: these are the modern trends.

WALK TALL WITHIN WALLS

Morality was lost long ago/not taught in schools so of course there's degeneracy with boys or girls.

Hidden pugnacity out of view: who else to abuse but a sibling, who else are they close to?

With three sisters it falls on the younger and that's Cinderella, an archetype from millennia.

If that trauma is now in my DNA I guess I'll be talking about this forever, it's the only way.

My emotions and truth were valid: what a revelation, I couldn't believe it after being silenced.

There is so much POWER in finally being able to break that silence, to shatter the interlopers.

The bullies who censored, gaslighted and manipulated us are dead, truth is here for good instead.

They're cowards--its why they ban together--while God's man's a loner, that's how he has power.

Women are worst looking innocent while they get others to do their dirty work on the ignorant.

IT HURTS TO BE MISJUDGED

Like it was with Jesus it hurts to be misjudged. It's a kind of identity theft way below God's best.

The ravenous wolves come off as sheep but wait a little while and you'll see the vicious creeps.

The trauma bonded lose boundaries and morals. There's a collapse of both and devastation is the result.

At first he came off as a beta male but getting closer his other side was sadistic and out of control.

WALK TALL WITHIN WALLS

Always talking about how good he is to others for brownie points but with you he gets outa joint.

I don't need to feel less than, again. I don't need to feel triangulated against, again. I'm #1 or none.

You can love another but still computers come first if you're this mental so it's separate not together.

Rejection re-arranges internal settings to abnormal, leaving us longing for the very thing that's lethal.

A deficient soul develops from not being loved completely or rejected and the void creates an addiction.

DESPERATE DESIRE FOR LOVE FILLING

There is a desperate desire to have that area filled and this desperation/panic turns off the intelligence.

This desperate love addiction turns down the voice of the holy spirit--discernment--as evil flows in.

The love addict then invests all of this energy into the first person that shows up, a great danger see.

When the new relationship turns toxic the victim is incapable of discerning abuse from loving.

Rejection and abuse has at this point become the norm. It sets a pattern as she inevitably spirals down.

The fatal love addict can't break free from the attraction to the very person causing the greatest harm.

Those who've not been loved properly develop toxic bond with rejectors because everything's corrective.

Chalk it up to a demon, that's all. Practice saying it so remorse can't take root cuz it's obstruction too.

WALK TALL WITHIN WALLS

THE HERO'S PATH IS CIRCUITOUS

The hero's path of personal development may seem circuitous to others but don't you bother.

The minute we die all these memories and entanglements vaporize and are meaningless. Think of this.

As long as you're grasping at straws and making stuff up as you go it's just too boring for me and slow.

While I wore myself out with work you wore yourself out with other women. It's not the same.

No one knows those people, it's mere fiction at this point so use it as a metaphor/don't get outa joint.

I coulda been killed. Yah but you weren't because God always shows up at the last minute it is told.

Rejection bruises the ego which compels the victim to return to more for mere human validation.

The Approval Trap is where you have a need for the rejector's approval, a weird thing indeed.

Wanting confirmation and acceptance from the very person who broke you is an example.

The person who broke you doesn't have the depth to cure you so forgive him/move up to higher crew.

"I need the person who did me wrong to apologize and accept me" is the most common trap today.

Many seek the ruler's favor but every man's judgement cometh from the Lord. Proverbs 29: 26

EMPTY TRADITION ROBS SELF-ESTEEM

WALK TALL WITHIN WALLS

Some traditions/false religions emptied her self-esteem bank and robbed her of her consciousness.

Screw the man for life and make everyone hate his guts and if they don't they're not part of the club.

I think you're a beta male who listens to his wife and it's disgusting. YOU lead your family buddy.

Anyone who keeps secrets is either illegal or immoral. Girl, never agree to stay on the "down low".

The first time I saw house it was "create thru elimination"--by removing all her frills it became a mansion.

You're no inferior man's secret. That guy's a clown to ask that of you, you must immediately dissociate.

One of the tricks of perverted male society is Flattery--because women are susceptible you see.

Women respond to WORDS. It's bound to impact em on a certain level but Queens are above the rabble.

The neighborhood seems totally quiet but any involvement or party turns your serene inner life into a riot.

I went to their party and instantly had to defend myself against subtle accusations/misperceptions.

The light they saw me in was so inferior all I did was work to change it to keep my head above water.

The first thing done in a concentration camp is depersonalization and it's a frightening thing.

NEIGHBORHOOD MISPERCEPTIONS

To be misjudged/mislabeled/miscast is spiritual amputation but can act as a catalyst and new foundation.

WALK TALL WITHIN WALLS

They misjudged me so badly I worked tenaciously to change the image until perfect/finished.

The neighborhood is TOTALLY QUIET. But that's only because I have absolutely no involvements.

I have have learned all this--my Ph.D. in the Streets--from porous boundaries and terrible experiences.

The "help" got involved with my personal life, eavesdropped, brought evil gossip, stole from me nonstop.

Thanksgiving neighborhood dinner: they were so cruel in a chamber of accusatory fools, never again sir.

To truly live one's OWN life is so difficult as the social world flows in demanding your full attention to it.

To gain full creative privacy and solitude to work you must first gain social muscle to manage the jerks.

It took me half my life to gain firm foundational boundaries but truthfully it was only all thru marriage.

As a woman I'm sensitive to words/signs but as a writer I'm far more so--subtle nuances between the lines.

They seem so innocuous but get involved and you'll be robbed and by their flying monkeys mobbed.

IF THEY COME WITH AN ARMY [FLYING MONKEYS]
/
If they come with an army, don't let em in! You're far too nonchalant about these little invasions.

A grand part of eldering is the world finally leaves you alone. Now, finally, your own star is shone.

Choosing what you want in life is second nature to normies but to trauma-bonded it's great difficulty.

WALK TALL WITHIN WALLS

Wicked men control weak women thru their insecurities: masterfully they give or withdraw flattery.

A woman has everything to gain by keeping her husband happy, healthy/in love with her homemaking.

I don't bake cookies like mommy it's about making home more inspiring, warming, creativity-producing.

Selecting the household music for the day: things like that, or a new dip I'd like you to try on a tray.

Careful of a man without vision. If all he has for you ma'am is flattery and you be lovin' it you're still a nut.

If your vision is in the penthouse and his is in the basement but you keep him cuz he flatters--think of it.

A woman sensitive to words/needing approval like a curse is fodder of novels/explains female neuroses.

People use words as battering rams--subtle nuances, polite cruelties, insidious nonverbal signs.

Oh, I could never go thru that again. That roller coster? No way, I can't even stand to recall back then.

The superior man senses danger just as the farmer does the future and that means to PREPARE.

Politics changes suddenly under new leadership see, coming thru meanspirited bureaucracy.

The wrong man will be the best sex but the queen never gets swept up, she's above all that stuff.

DATING PROCESS VETS THE DROSS

During the dating process she is teaching a man how to respect her by the way she respects herself.

WALK TALL WITHIN WALLS

If he's always calling you last minute he's always thinking about you last. Learn these lessons Lass.

A man's use of time determines his priorities. He will make a date on Sunday for the next Saturday.

Never make a man your priority until he's clearly made you HIS. If you're a secret/last minute it's a DIS.

If he keeps calling at the last second you're showing he's your priority before him proving you're his.

Kings love women with boundaries--who won't change their plans with the girls at the last minute, see.

Never shrink your profile to accommodate an inferior man's intimidation. Don't get small to fit his thing.

By you cutting off self to adapt to him, he's comfortable but you are compressed then illness is next.

It was uncomfortable for me to even fit into such a small space. Ultimately I became the craziest.

With total solitude the insane emotional bedlam of the gossiping grapevine became tranquil/quiet.

Cain and Abel: Rather than expanding himself to be equal he wanted only to kill him--how typical.

The more I know the more I see it as a Human Jungle. If unprepared you're bound for big trouble.

Why so much on narcissists? Well cuz that's one of the few topics you aren't banned if you discuss.

He hated on his brother but had the opportunity to do the same thing--isn't that just like human beings?

IF HE HATES YOUR SUCCESS WITHDRAW MISS

WALK TALL WITHIN WALLS

If he hates your success he thinks poorly of himself [not enough man for you] and is unpredictable Miss.

So girl when you find a little man who's intimidated by you let him move on and you move on too.

Stop trying to find a man just cuz you're 55 and marry yourself to your vision-- THAT is happiness.

I pursued a rejector 'til I lost the vision God had put in me pastor but now I'm back as a creative factor.

Stay strong and wait for better. Never settle for lesser or decades are lost to the destroyer/messer.

Fulfill God's purpose in your life then wait for Him to send the right besides you--to accentuate/no strife.

Pneumaticity means: You leave space for what God has prepared for you then it will be sent soon.

They panic, fill their lives with wrong men then when the right ones pass by they are fully preoccupied.

With wrong men you think "I don't know why" but space was always filled when Mr. good passed by.

The punishments for not being patient enough to wait are great--like your best wasted for decades.

AMERICANS WERE DECENT: THINK OF THE ANIMALS!

I loved animals but he was cruel, that was his culture. His presence ruined my life/the thought makes me shudder.

You may think multiculturalism is about great food. Hah--it's about collision with the rude, crude and cruel.

The culture clash created a psychosis in those with emotional sensitivities. The hyper-sensitives/old ladies.

WALK TALL WITHIN WALLS

Because of this lifelong thorn in my side, I learned all about the effects of multiculturalism and the snide.

Please dear Lord help the dogs and cats. For we're being invaded by cultures who hate/kill em and it's bad.

Through progressives a new moral system was imposed on us: i.e. no morals save the evils of globalists.

Immigration: Should be one at a time, those who benefit us. Now it's floods and many want to kill us.

Set-up job: a vicious witch going to bat for globalists who'll do anything to end Trump, just like that.

Women: Don't be fools. If Hillary got in, in comes the Muslim masses to debase you (it'd be cruel).

Brexit should inspire the west. It can be done: break the block of the big banks and return to nationalism.

The Clinton Foundation won't pay women equally. That makes sense being funded by Islamic royalty.

They block nationalism because they're bought off by globalists. Watch or your country will drift off.

The elites in state communism are bureaucrats who don't produce anything-- therefore you have poverty.

RICH LEFTIST SNOBS ENJOY WALLS

If she got in, prepare to be flooded with the entire third world within a month- -a Tsunami /a bunch.

Trump can get rid of them quickly. He's the master problemsolver: they're outa here/we'll be giddy.

Wait until they start killing your dogs and cats and then Sharia police come to the door for them: facts.

WALK TALL WITHIN WALLS

Liberals have a sort of romantic notion of the middle east. Face the facts people it is terrible, please!

Open-border progressives have no idea what it's like flooded with antithetical cultures: A blight.

Hillary you say to accept them. Hillary they marry children, they stone women/gays and you say "it's all ok".

Unlimited migration is tantamount to world communism and that is the goal of the UN and the likes of Hillary Clinton.

They aren't like us! They are immoral, cruel, disorderly, entitled, ruthless and they hate us: God help us!

Just look at all the coal and natural gas God has given us--to be independent and free of fuss.

We must stand up to the government-media complex: No war with Russia-- Trump-Putin will fix.

The Catholics, Baptists and Lutherans are making billions from savages they let in and this isn't sin?

Even Mormons want open borders! The churches go crazy with pity as they bus in moochers and the lazy.

Can't you see she's their operative, their totalitarian under left cover? Please...stop her.

Islam encroaches incrementally: First it's fashion then get rid of your dogs like they're the enemy.

BRINGING IN THE *HORRIBLY* BACKWARDS

They're bringing in the most horribly backwards (80% military age) men to trash the renaissance/the west.

Relocate, prepare, grow food, make connections ok? Make decisions for the coming time (either way).

WALK TALL WITHIN WALLS

They behave when held back. When bowed and cowed to, they become a raging fire/things go black.

You must kill it for It's an invader, a conquistador--it will kill and torture you. War is the Christian thing to do.

Their theology is satanic. It can't be anything else, there's a pattern how demons act and they're proud of it.

Renaissance: they didn't have it, we did. That's why they're crass, gross, trashy and violent.

On nationalism: The more local the more me-ism. The more global the more loco/spiritual terrorism.

Globalism is concentration of wealth in the elite and our total dependency. The solution: prosperity.

Globalism is cronyism while nationalism (by cutting taxes on the middle class) is money explosion!

Although we feel sympathy we can't let everyone into our country, we must think of our own out of money.

The disgusting "loving" liberals, so misled. Care more about immigrants though they want us dead.

What makes the globalists most upset is patriots who are awake. Globalists in government: snakes.

The NWO goal is to de-industrialize populations and divide and conquer by making you dumb and poor.

Globalists pay thugs big bucks to obstruct and it's all against Trump since he wants us flush with great luck.

GLOBALISTS HATE FREE ECONOMIES

The globalists don't want an open/free economy so they're shutting down the Trump phenomenon, see?

WALK TALL WITHIN WALLS

Vetting: Let's take people who are good for a country who cares: bright, educated and won't need welfare

Globalism a one-sided screw job and Trump's gonna reverse it to what America means: just our thing.

Bring back the incredible American dynamo: No taxes for working people/not letting globalists sell us out (evil).

Renaissance: they didn't have it, we did. That's why they're crass, gross, trashy and violent.

Elites have jumbo jets, mansions and 50 mistresses but you have nothing: that's the plan by the bosses.

Globalists admit their system is austerity. Trump is proud to say our system will be prosperity.

Globalists (Agenda 21) seek to ban "single family dwellings" so we end up in ghettos with few belongings.

As Hillary and globalism fizzles, so too communism because it all goes together and is so dismal.

Crony capitalism is: picking winners. They wanna make you poor to control you through corporate tyrants.

Globalism and the left's had their foot on our necks. Take that tax off and we shoot up/explode in progress.

Cruel to women, children, animals: not a religion but a political system of conquest and domination, amen.

Climate change is one big scam. Whenever you hear it, think globalism and cronyism: money to be had.

Globalists want all the wealth, power and innovation but they're against our progress as a nation.

STATE'S RIGHTS MEANS ANTI-GLOBALIST

WALK TALL WITHIN WALLS

The biggest block to globalism is state's rights. That means prosperity not dumb like mice.

All because he wants to turn the economy back on they hate him, wanna kill him/call for assassination.

To control us globalists want us poor and dumb. The only solution to that is thriving nationalism.

If worried about women, blacks and gays getting executed--it's not about Trump, in Islam it's rooted.

Just look at these dumbed down zombies, filled with esoteric BS by commies and professor cronies.

If Hillary wins we'll go right into borderless world communism and corruption far worse than Obamaism.

It's not just about saving the American dream but also Western Civilization and its dying nations.

They aren't nice but inherently and consciously evil people who want to hurt you and your family--believe me.

Trump needs to ban halal (cruel slaughter). Muslims think nothing of it even if their wife or daughter.

30,000 scientists see Global Warming as a scam to make money for a few and Donald thinks this too.

Mexico wants US money funneling into Mexico. So of course they want no borders: no need to fix cartels.

Obama wants to pardon the dreamers--another word for illegals breaking the law--as our new leaders.

DUMPING ILLEGALS FOR FREE VACATIONS

Dumping illegals for free-cations in Arizona/California in response to no jail space: Obama to be erased.

WALK TALL WITHIN WALLS

Globalists are allied with China to bring US/Russia down. They formed the EU to suck it dry/take it's crown.

Our tolerance for global government which is tax exempt and above their laws is low cuz we're in the know.

They gutted our working class while establishing a middle class in Asia: the elite plan to steer it all through China.

Increasingly we're abridging our freedoms so as not to offend savages. Pamela Geller

France is the sinking ship meme whose life purpose is to warn others, maybe?

Actually inviting people in who want to conquer you and paying them for it.

Sanctuary cities: Protect criminal aliens, lose federal money. It's your decision. -the federal government.

I know what can happen letting strangers in your house.

Divorce starts with porous boundaries. If it were just you two youd've stayed happy.

Cling to God, guns, bible, traditions. Mass unvetted immigration is immoral, irrational and suicidal man.

Having an opinion is Islamaphobic and it's wrong to be scared?

With Canada sliding into Islamo-communism we should thank God our man is smart/logical--why we love him.

There is a problem in Islam and the problem is: we can't talk about the problem. Pamela Geller

There's a vicious war raging across the world and all we can talk about is backlashaphobia. Pamela Geller

VICTORY WAS THROUGH TERROR

I am victorious through terror. Mohammed

WALK TALL WITHIN WALLS

I got so used to injustice/false weights (prejudice) that Stockholm Syndrome took over (caved in to the dis).

It's not that they love immigrants but that they hate Trump.

Our sense of what's normal is gone.

Our world as we knew it is crumbling due to the myth of multiculturalism and this is the awful culmination.

Bill Clinton knocked down doors to deport illegals, Trump isn't but he's the target of accusations/anecdotals.

Anti-American/nationalism took hold in the sixties supplanted by the utopian vision of ONE world/no differences.

They just can't accept all cultures are different. Hypnotized to see "all is good" they can't see: they're not friends.

Truth is the new hate speech. Pamela Geller

How morally depraved, vacuous, cynical, dangerous and empty these new world order systems are.

Love it or leave it. The anti-American garbage on TV is 100% bought and paid for--believe it, see it.

Most creative needs highest walls.

Ruin or Rome: borders gone, barbarians flow in.

They know they wanna kill us but are flooding us anyway: vicious.

The battle is between good and evil in Trump's new "principled realism."

POLITICAL CORRECTNESS FOR SAKE OF ISLAM

Political correctness is the handmaiden of Islamic terror. Michelle Malkin

WALK TALL WITHIN WALLS

We have been liberated from a tyranny that would have ramped up fast but God had His own plans: destiny!

There's an explosion of not "right wing bigotry" but rather nationalism, common sense and freedom.

Just hate America: With liberals any time of authoritarianism is fine--aren't we tired of debauched swine?

How liberals to launch globalist corporate system: Limit debate, target dissidents and dismiss them.

It's a world revolution occurring everywhere: not being bullied by political correctness anymore.

What is globalism? It's worldwide corporate tyranny not some great, exotic and colorful one "community".

Globalist libs can't compete with Western values of human rights so they boost Islam and it's not right.

What does Islam and Liberalism have in common? They wanna dismantle the West thinking it's rotten.

Ivanka's pushing open borders and globalism? Merkel's new best friend? Fake news I'm hopin

If the dems go radical Islam they'll co-exist with ISIS and be equally dangerous.

Instead of fighting the real enemy which is radical Islam they create a false enemy which is Russia.

Peace is profitable so of course we're joining Russian forces to fight ISIS.

Say what you want about em, we need partners in fighting ISIS--that's all that matters: killing ISIS.

Socialism's where you vote tyranny in, communism's where your freedom's just taken.

GREEN IS THE NEW RED

WALK TALL WITHIN WALLS

Green is the new red--it's communism.

A nation with out borders is like a house without walls--it collapses. Democrats wants this: what asses.

Immigrants in food inspection so they find cats used in Chinese buffets across the nation.

The liberals for open borders are responsible for the terror.
Coulter: Rome burns and Nero worries about Pyrophobia.

Fat-shaming isn't sexist, FGM is you sadists.

U.N. decides who comes into our country, not us--according to what Obama signed, the louse.

Don't tell me slavery brands America as bad. Because along with the KKK it was democrats who did that.

How to radically re-engineer society: Let Islam in the door--loving what we abhor/trashing what we adore.

Sanctuary Cities: Trump is gonna get 'em and deport the Muslims so now liberals are showing desperation.

Globalism is a worldwide system of austerity: people being poor, ignorant and played off against each other.

The globalists cannot co-exist with an open free market society so they graft in Islam for needed tyranny.

Globalism is: Third wave corporate colonialism establishing a planetary above-the-law dictatorship.

They wanna make us all one race and play third world populations off against the West (the best).

Islam has called for Vehicular Jihad in the West: Running em down with cars, vans and trucks is best.

FOX'S SPEEDBUMPS AND DETRACTORS

WALK TALL WITHIN WALLS

Too many speedbumps and detractors on Fox. That's why half get their news here on FB though much is blocked.

Trump our savior: It was as if it opened up a portal to another world which we had shut under a monster.

It's globalism, and Islam is the operating system. Muslim welfare seekers destroying host, amen.

Border Patrol: zero tolerance coming soon. On his very first day we'll start to feel safe and more immune.

Globalists--the illuminati--are tapped into the deepest, darkest evil forces on the earth, trashing our worth.

The globalists are into the lowest form of witchcraft we know, and it's their insidious line we must tow?

It's a corporate global government with a technocracy to control people through a pagan worldview: occult, evil.

Elites: Pizzagate shows their goal is a cashless society and pedophilia as they seek to legalize 12 perversions.

Every time the elite try to take over something happens to prevent it--a techtonic shift going worldwide quickly.

Globalism means: Italy is no more, France is gone, England just folklore. God wants uniqueness galore.

If neighbor watches mainstream news it's state-run media and they're dumb as rocks and angry at me too.

Constitutional Carry is open or concealed. Our 2nd amendment rights don't disappear crossing state lines ya know.

Calling them "fake" they shut down news sites not because they're fake but because they expose the fake.

LOVING TRUMP IS THE LITMUST TEST

WALK TALL WITHIN WALLS

Loving Trump is the litmus test, the barometer cuz if you don't we have absolutely nothing in common.

Facebook censuring has begun and nothing's happening, no more fun, can't talk about Muslims or guns.

Being chemically sensitive I don't know what's worse: the symptoms or the isolation (seen as fakin').

For the first time I wanted to rush the Christmas season—couldn't wait for Trump to take over for so many reasons.

Many warriors just wanna rape and kill. There are no ideals and elites pay to make western civilization nil.

Liberals instinctively hate everything that made America great.

We're one mile away, closing in on you. You can either stay in the bunker or escape but your days are few.

You watch lame news and think you're intellectuals. Anyone with a brain can see your end is here, fools.

Dynamo president is filled with energy, strength, smarts they don't have. They can't stand it: envy from the bad.

American ain't perfect but it's the best nation the world has ever seen.

The liberals hate the military but created horrible wars: such contradictions we've learned to abhor.

Why the absurd Russian election scam? To trigger continuity of government emergency (kill, imprison) plans.

They even say Merkel's losing due to Russians--not that she brought in 2 million Jihadis to crush em.

Recount shows Trump won much more massively than we thought and they're panicking on every front.

TRUMP'S TURNED PROSPERITY BACK ON

WALK TALL WITHIN WALLS

Trump's turning prosperity back on after artificially turned off. Commies hate this and so they scoff.

All those regs were an admitted plan to de-industrialize us. They're that evil and that's why they fuss.

Globalists getting their hit teams ready to kill Trump, claiming fraud election blamed on a Russian coup.

Globalists (EU) to Italy: "Oh, you wanna pull out? We'll send our military in" and crazy stuff like that.

CIA and State Dept. censorship went through today. Shutting us all down, we're allowed nothing more to say.

Calling fraud for the election: The CIA would do that--a rogue anti-American organization from 1947.

No one likes the Islamicists enslaving women but the left is allied with them--it's bizarre coming from "stars".

The Russians kicked the globalist oligarchs out: they're nationalists! Putin has the same view as us patriots.

To pseudo-intellectual liberals: You can't take that you've lost so now you're making an ass of yourself.

Can't put the genie back in the bottle: the dynamic human spirit that refuses to submit (so give up, twits).

Not gonna submit to you fake ivy league nobodies anymore. So go back where you came from, bores.

Your parents produced something but you are soulless jokes that nobody likes so you're u nder the yoke.

The left sees the American flag as racism.

NFL WERE GLOBALISTS TOOLS YOU FOOLS

The NFL is a tool of the globalists destroying itself.

WALK TALL WITHIN WALLS

You're not gonna stop the Trump Train, the manifestation of populism and the old-fashioned manly way.

Trump-phoria: Highest level of confidence from individuals for innovation and new jobs in America.

Rome had Golden Ages of jobs, freedom and prosperity. Trump wants to preside over largess, certainly.

Globalism/Common Core: consensus panels, groupthink, majority rule, compromise--things I despise.

Let invaders in, you'll have to do things their way. Liberals say no-borders, leading us to a horrible day.

He was a warrior: killing, looting, raping, enslaving. They follow his example, doing what he taught, hating.

"You don't get it unless you die". That hopelessness spurs the ruthless acts whereas we have hope in fact.

The elites don't want purpose-driven people they want cogs that fit into algorithms and create schisms.

NATIONALISM IS NOT RACISM

Nationalism is not racism--it's awakening to the corporate global government, get it?

If God be for us, who can be against us? And if God's against us, we're done: toast, the end, bust.

They're making their move, Trump's the counter-coup and their fall's imminent too.

They went too far and that's how tyrants end up falling. They shoot high then God appears and it's bye-bye.

These liberals cannot function when the light is on them. That's why they hate Infowars: shut up vermin.

WALK TALL WITHIN WALLS

It wasn't Russians influencing the election, but Saudi and China who openly said they gave her millions.

The EU openly bragged about financing anti-Trump hacks in the election, but oh-no, it's the "Russians".

ELITES PUT BLINDERS AND GAGS ON AMERICANS

Elites put blinders and gags on Americans, suppressing them by teaming up with any authoritarians.

False dogma ruins their lives, but they create much trouble before doing themselves in with bad deeds/lies.

"Conspiracy theorist" is the name for anyone who's informed by the corrupt U.N. of the third world.

Clinton/Soros biggest criminal org in world and presidency is key to controlling it, by making Electors flip.

They're not gonna walk away from this position they've worked all their lives for--expect big things galore.

They push through a bad order, do nothing for a week or two: When we're distracted they lower the boom.

If they don't like what you say, regardless of the truth, they will shut you down. Persevere, don't backdown!

The globalists are scum, degenerates: Look how they turned radical Jihadis loose on the whole planet.

It's freezing--but what about Global Warming? They've changed all that to "climate change" warnings.

Foreigners got rich by bleeding America dry. Politicians did nothing but now we'll be first so to you: bye bye.

Don't want global we want local! So get you're mundane, evil, colorless crap outa here, it's loco.

WALK TALL WITHIN WALLS

INTENSE NATIONALISM FROM SUDDEN REVELATIONS

Intense nationalism comes from revealed corporate globalism, a scientific authoritarianism.

Patriotism will be taught to our children very strongly and that will bring jobs back to America. Pres. Trump

It's a system: big corporations don't give sponsorship if you want freedom, justice, sovereignty, or aren't evil.

We're the Kings of free market renaissance in our heyday--wanna bring that back cuz that's our future, ok?

Total mind control putting us in a catatonic basket case learned helpless Stockholm Syndrome: "racist"

We don't communicate with each other since we wanna be correct and nothing's correct, everything's bad.

They call us "racist" and "terrorist" and when we respond back, we're "mean".

Communists always say "peace" which means "stop fighting us".

"Peace" means to give up and accept communism and concentration camps.

America is experiencing the highest confidence, ever. The statistics are mind-blowing (Trump's so clever).

You may have to transcend the lower rung (original family/friends) to get to the higher who will not offend.

A country is judged by what kind of life it gives to the common man. Rich people live well everywhere, brahman.

I support the wall, I support the ban.

Declared: resettle them there, not here. For every ONE settled here, twelve can be resettled there.

WALK TALL WITHIN WALLS

The means of fighting wars abroad will be brought back as tyranny at home. The Founding Fathers.

THEY WANT US RENTERS FOR CONTROL

They want us all renters to consolidate control. They jack up power prices, take property and shut down coal.

I don't care if you worship a stone--just don't stone me with it. Pamela Geller

Globalists seek to get rid of sovereignty then merge smaller states into superstates under global treaties.

China buys Hollywood (we see propaganda): all six houses. California's dying and these are the processes.

Adversity makes men, prosperity makes monsters. Victor Hugo

The model of freedom in America is the best hope for everybody.

The United Nations is veiled anti-semitism.

Geo Soros funds American tragedies, has destroyed 15 countries violently and 30 by plunging their currencies.

Italy's gone our way: the anti-populist has lost! The globalists are panicking at this revolution/our new boss.

Bitter clingers (to God, guns, country and liberty) unite!

Freedom, liberty, justice for all: Renaissance thought. That's what they don't have, not by a long shot.

You have "democratic republics" all over the world--China, Cuba--and that means tyranny runs the globe.

It's a corporate democracy under world communism--we just escaped this by banishing Hillary Clinton.

If we don't understand the basics we won't ever recognize classical tyranny when it's in our face.

WALK TALL WITHIN WALLS

"STARS" MEANS SATAN'S IN THERE

National Academy of Television Arts and Sciences is Satan spelled backwards--see that about "stars".

Cultural relativism compels extremism so they get dirtier and dirtier to be superior and that's elitism.

You either come to our country to be like us or to change us. If the latter: stay outa our country, klutz.

Everything we stand for is antithetical to devotion of Islam. NO freedom of speech, dress, guns or religion.

Bring them to their region and protect them there, not here. Heed warnings of their killings and be a bear.

Bible: Peace, love, freedom of choice. Koran: Subjection, violence, force.

They populate, infiltrate, agitate and wage war. See it as a fire: identify source, contain it, beat it down.

Libs are doing everything to undermine our landslide, cuz he's appointed patriots/anti-globalists with pride.

Two-party dictatorship engaged in insider trading. Trump's the first breath of fresh air, break from despair.

The corruption gets more emboldened until they go so far the public wakes up/it's all over for them.

Like a phoenix from the fire of hell our republic is rising again. Alex Jones

The globalist gang rape is over. Alex Jones

America didn't need to take over: we won through our shine, not as controllers.

Radical Islamic Terrorism is the Cancer.

WALK TALL WITHIN WALLS

Come together and we'll be protected by our military, law enforcement and most importantly, God. -Pres. Trump

PRAY FOR THE SPIRIT OF JUSTICE

May the spirit of justice and prosperity be turned loose.

Nationalism = prosperity. Globalism = poverty.

We are not living in Capitalism but the age of Global Corporatism.

One of God's punishments is not just natural disasters but also suddenly being surrounded by strangers.

Globalists and liberals wanted to flood us with millions who hate us and you were on the Clinton bus?

The biggest political realignments in history and it's happening all over the world at the same time: superiority!

Independence: We're gonna take back our freedom, property and self-governance from a small globalists cabal.

Globalists are scrambling across the world as their stranglehold on humanity becomes looser, and looser. Alex Jones

Since just one can do so much damage, obviously we can't let one in.

Globalism (like Clintons) wanted to take away our ability to direct our own destiny and you voted for Hillary?

All the globalists/liberals can do is lie because their's is the father of lies.

It's historic: The forces of tyranny trying to stop innovation, bringing in a dark age of oppression: we're gone.

"Think globally, act locally" means to understand the enemy.

LIBERTY *ALWAYS* TRUMPS TYRANNY

Liberty always trumps tyranny if we decide we want it. Alex Jones

WALK TALL WITHIN WALLS

Why was Michelle frowning the whole time? Because they were a cult put in power by globalists to divide.

Hussein/Hillary created them first and millions got hurt, but we'll destroy ISIS from the face of the earth.

Of course the Russians pulled away from the same mega-banks--the left sees that as collusion? No thanks.

Hollywood and the globalists are a bunch of anti-family, anti-Christian weirdo freaks who hate the Unique.

Stop abusing America with your own personal leftist mind control. Alex Jones

They wanna mount our head on the wall: kill the U.S./suck it dry pursuant to world government, that's all.

The media's fall shows a rejection of globalism, elitism and east coast snobbery/anti-liberty socialism.

GLOBALIST WORLD ENGINEERS

The globalist social engineers are the worst of the worst: totally bloodthirsty and twisted (read all I've listed).

Magnificent spirit of the individual totally defeats the spirit of control and poverty of Hollywood/globalists.

Hollywood's the culmination of a sick premise since the sixties: there is no God/His Unique are odd.

Pope: "evil sees borders and barriers" and "Islam isn't violent". Has church been taken over--can we be silent?

Liberals don't believe in borders, barriers or privacy (except their own), bring all their friends into your home.

One world government brings in incompatible religions and says "it must be accepted or you're arrested".

WALK TALL WITHIN WALLS

The west is the best, that's why they move here--bringing their worst, creating ghettos that are cursed.

Americana reboot: Power back to the people. What we've been through with the traitors in government, so evil!

GLOBALISTS HIJACKED OUR COUNTRY

Globalists hijacked our country and now we've had a coup to restore it. You'll feel the difference, believe it.

Globalists want the American Renaissance/restoration of the republic to fail and that's why these women wail!

These women are being globalist-used but since they don't know history they're willing and even amused.

Women! The globalists want you to be alone and desperate--this is just a way to control you (share this)!

Immigrants waiting 10 yrs. to be legal but dems won't allow it--want a poor permanent underclass, illigit.

Americana culture will make us dominate worldwide, bringing prosperity to all in another landslide.

If we work hard and are good and moral Jan.20 will be the new July 4th. Will all good men now come forth?

Globalism's designed to make us poor. Donald Trump is not out to get you-- give him a chance, and soar!

Globalists shut factories with out a thought of the millions left behind. A boomtown near me closed all mines.

The wealth was ripped from their homes and redistributed all across the world. President Donald Trump

"America first" simply means: no more being slaves to globalists.

THE CIA RUNS THE "WOMEN'S MARCHES"

WALK TALL WITHIN WALLS

Women's marches are run by the CIA hijacked by foreign powers.

It's their culture, a religion: Leftist cultural weirdos/twisted ideology (has cohesion through social psychology).

Glitz and glamour of the superior: we don't care what you think sir.

Obama was trying to consolidate the country and give the business to his friends--that's what globalism IS.

Betrayal of Israel at the United Nations. Trying to ruin relations with our most important ally and former superpower.

China opens two (dirty) coal mines a week while ours (clean) are shut down. Global warming is America's crackdown.

The Time Warner stock is plunging--it's anti-family, anti-gun and globalist-- so stock-dumping into nothing.

True Western liberalism: not fake (fascist, globalist neo-liberalism) but returning to what made us great.

Russia is our natural ally in the fight against radical Islam.

The boot-in-the-face is pacified with hedonism.

"Children" are coming in but that's defined < 31 years old (it's spin).

They want us to surrender our own identity and God-created diversity to a unipolar world they call "diversity".

The dems wanted immigration to change the demographics so they'd be in power for 100 years: forget it.

They let foreign floods in not to change things ethnically but politically-- voters, no matter the tragedies.

LEFT: POWER FROM RHETORIC AND RIOTS

WALK TALL WITHIN WALLS

Left is so used to power from rhetoric and riots they don't realize the world's shifted and continue to deny it.

To the degree that the outer world is profane and secular, the home must be holy and cloistered. G.C. Dilsaver

People won't listen to you because they won't listen to Me, for all are hardened and obstinate. Ezekiel 3: 7-9

The media has a vicious hatred of America, thinking cuz they're in a hive with traitors they're invincible, oh yah?

In their echo chamber they think they'll get away with it, but just watch as they do themselves in--bring it!

For 50 years we've been waiting/watching as you did your evil thing and now we've shot up like a box spring.

Trump's gonna publish weekly crimes of illegals--absolutely! A major cover up has occurred, profusely.

2 biggest risks: Islam and feminism, who like each other a lot. What strange contradictions: think about that.

They don't "come here to work", idiots. Look at actual data for a change: immigrants use welfare most, hideous.

Trump's orders: only a small beginning. Daddy's gonna do what it takes despite your maudlin/childish crying.

1970's: California schools were the best in the nation. Now they're the worst in the world--any connection?

Chemtrails: headache, vertigo, dizziness, nausea, carsick feel, depression, fatigue, flue--is this you?

Clever: Putting out false info so we debate it for weeks while they fight against foes of New World Order.

MEXICO IS CARTELS AND TORTURE

WALK TALL WITHIN WALLS

Mexico is famous for cartels and massive torture, now part of the system. And we can't have a wall? Twisted

It's not a Muslim but a terrorist ban.

We must undo all that's been done to us by Hussein--flooding us with aliens, enemies and the diseased.

Of course they want sanctuary cities how else could old bitties stay in power like Pelosi and her leftist cronies?

Things will change rapidly as border agents switch to sanctuary cities and demand work papers today.

It's so simple: he just turns off the spigot and withdraws federal funding. How great he is with stroke of a pen.

Billions of dollars grifted from illegal alien programs just in Frisco. The theft is beyond belief in this fiasco.

California stole benefits for taxpayers and gave it to invaders but it all changes by turning off spigot in a minute.

TRUMP TOOK OUR NATION BACK

Trump's taking our nation back from the hordes who overran us. So globalist pawns hate him (having a fuss).

Went through hell for 8 years but then a man came along who noted what we wanted and delivered undaunted!

Barry brought trainloads of mothers with children saying we had to take care of them and churches chimed in.

Invaders took everything that should go to America's poor: the elderly and more.

We endured insults from liberal vultures: "How dumb can you get to believe in borders, language and culture!"

WALK TALL WITHIN WALLS

Where do you think this money came from? It was diverted from the veterans.

It's almost scary: "we can't take that much winning, please stop" and our dear President said "sorry, can't".

Mr. President, we can't take this much winning--please stop! "No, we have a million more bombs to drop".

GLOBALISTS IN DEATH THROES

Globalists are in death throes, panicking at Trump right now who got a standing ovation at the CIA: wow.

The globalists wanted us disempowered and dependent. Trump says no— you're the power and he meant it.

Trump's message was like sunlight to vampires--the antithesis of the New World Order--and we're on fire!

Open you heart to patriotism and there is no prejudice. Donald Trump

We've defended nation's borders while refusing to defend our own. We built up their militaries while ours: none.

The servile minions of evil enjoy wielding power but the strong don't want to enslave people/make them cower.

May never know the cause of weird disease but it's usually a mal-adaptation to "X" foisted on us from sleaze.

Our guy's delivering, delivering: bombing ISIS is green-lighted after being banned by the previous skinny man.

Our man started bombing ISIS within one hour of being president. He even captured the head guy (a rodent).

Like Nineveh given a reprieve, we're about to go to the next level of taking over planet cuz God has granted it.

WALK TALL WITHIN WALLS

Feminazis with hijabs shout "Allahu Akbar" at Islamist-backed women's march and it's for women? Take no part!

The evil (Saudis) buy their way through gov but our guy won't play that game and that's why America's reclaimed.

Trade deals were unelected, a transfer of our sovereignty, they stunk and were unconstitutional—that's all.

THEY ACTUALLY HATE PROSPERITY

They hate prosperity--they'd better hate it since they won't get anything with those worthless degrees.

Globalism is a huge unelected oppressive tyranny using these chumps to do their dirty work, really.

We're excited by the relaunch of America as globalism falls apart, designed to bring her down/to thwart.

Trump's America is about to take over the world not with corporate chiefs but the wealth of our ideas.

They crushed non-radical Islamists like Saddam, Kadafi, Assad--and installed radicals like Saudis, oh God!

They're bombing ISIS with the Russians. Trump is so great I can't even keep track: he's so impressive!

Trump bombed ISIS within one hour of being president, as soon as Massis confirmed the tide had turned!

Within one hour the USAF was green-lighted after being blocked. It's happening, I'm stoked.

After 8 years of being blocked and stuck ISIS is crushed--bad luck!

Sharia Law pushers managed women's march. This was not about empowering women, but a scourge.

WALK TALL WITHIN WALLS

The west is freedom for women, spoils women, puts em on a pedestal and they're bitching at white men?

The left's merged with Islam, believing they're the muscle taking over for them! Lord, please come!

THEIR PSYCHOLOGY: BRING DOWN THE WEST

Their psychology is to bring down the west. It's not about race, sex or color but to disempower the best.

They do not fight real evils (like communism) they fight made-up ones.

They're desperate to keep racial politics in control as they indoctrinate minorities into racism/this hole.

They wanna keep the spotlight for without it would be depression, nihilism, emptiness even suicide.

"Multicultural" actually means "multi-racial" because to liberals if they're all white it's nothing special.

Multiculturalism in neighborhoods causes bad problems but to liberals that's irrelevant.

Endless democides, cultural suicides/slaughterhouses of the 21st century were the worst in history.

The democides of the last century were the set up for what we have now, an imminent tragedy.

Europe is done--it's finished--but it may take a long time. Nigel Farage

To libs the English, Irish and French aren't "multicultural" cuz they're all white and thus not rational.

The white Christians ended slavery but nevertheless now they are the only group blamed for slavery.

Trump has compassion but could not allow Obama's illegal and dangerous amnesty program to continue.

WALK TALL WITHIN WALLS

DACA was illegal, a scam to flood us for cheap labor/a voting block but they call us racist still.

ARROGANT CREEPS PAID BY GLOBALIST SCUM

Arrogant creeps bought off by globalist scum, mere pawns--but history will record the savior TRUMP.

Young Americans have dreams too. POTUS

Antifa's into weapons like ISIS, can't distinguish.

Americans are worried about chain immigration: let one in, they all come.

Crazy liberals say the more immigrants the better off we are. They don't care about us already here.

Knowing they can't win elections they simply cut/paste whole populations.

Despite Trump in, the liberals are heavily entrenched in the bureaucracy, continuing the insanity.

They actually think we're progressing as a society including invasion stuff. The utopians, mere fluff.

It's scary how these smiling feminists (teeth bared) say "open the borders" and the more the better.

NWO wants to cloud the lines between men and women, right and wrong. It wants obedience, not the headstrong.

Great tragedies are visited on people as a warning to wake up. God works in mysterious ways, look up.

To deny Christian roots (the basis of Western civilization) leads to horrid demoralization and demotion.

Without moral values (formed over millennia) people lose their dignity and become brutes. Vladimir Putin

WALK TALL WITHIN WALLS

Deport anyone who believes in Shariah cuz it's incompatible with western civilization/America.

If God rose Trump up He'll also keep him safe. Pray.

PULL THE PLUG, TURN OFF THE SPIGOT!

Pull the plug, turn off the spigot: We don't care if you call us bigots.

The majority wants border security and extreme vetting despite what the fake polls are saying. Pres. Trump

They celebrate death and worship destruction. Is this not just Islam but also feminism, liberalism and globalism?

Glorifying, washing the feet of, throwing flowers at immigrants they don't even know: that's democrats, whoa!

Go Trump: Globalists are out of options as populist movements are gaining steam and coming against them.

Ours is the God of separation and order and that speaks of boundaries and borders.

Hate him: Trump's repudiating multiculturalism, open bordersism, cultural relativism, globalism and third worldism.

They act like a sovereign nation doesn't have the right to control it's own borders--they wanna let em all in.

Europe's Stockholm Syndrome: they hope to convert to a weird socialist communist globalist form of Islam.

Trump's a giant wrecking ball against evil but minions of the system don't know what to do so destroy/steal.

Soros opened Europe to 5 million with 85% military age men. He is committed to evil/bringing us down, amen.

Soros doubled funding of insurrection a week after election: goal of cashless society/one world government.

WALK TALL WITHIN WALLS

GLOBALISTS CONSOLIDATE NO MATTER WHAT

Let's not make it about puppets Biden and Trudeau but the issues bringing the entire world close.

To tell the global elites: We won't take your stolen wealth we just want you to stop trying to kill us.

As long as globalists can consolidate power they don't care: they'll work with people like communist China.

Obama said "power to the people" then unemployment for black people doubled: How bloody cold blooded.

Not a Muslim ban but on certain wartorn countries. That's cuz of social hypnotism, it gets on em like disease.

Let em all in: When will states stop suiciding their citizens?

We have the warning: we see Europe. That's what Donald Trump is trying to save us from, so cheer up.

THE SOROS JUDGES

Why wasn't it illegal and involving judges when Obama was bringing trainloads/millions in unvetted?

Media repeats "Muslim Ban" or "religious test" and it's a complete LIE but we're pushing back through our guy.

85% of Muslim-filled nations were NOT on the list so just shut up CNN/fake news you've been properly dissed.

Trump's "divorced from reality" says CNN cuz he said there's been terror attacks they haven't reported again.

It's just common sense not to let people and their friends into your home like the bothersome or unknown.

Our only salvation is a Muslim ban cuz they wanna kill us man.
Hijra is Muslim colonization through immigration: migrate to dominate.

WALK TALL WITHIN WALLS

If we don't stop it now we're doomed. Cuz like Europe once they're here it's too late and we're consumed.

The mark of a weak silly woman is letting evil into her house. She must learn lesson of boundaries/the louse.

After learning boundaries you must suffer memories of the years of not having them and wow it hurts man.

Kick em out: They hate us, wanna kill us, seek to supplant us and feel superior--isn't that enough?

Many have to be invaded in their homes to know what this is all about. Before then they say "love em all".

ELITES WANT NEO-FEUDALISM AGAIN

Elites want us fallen back to neo-feudalism where every culture was the same (differences bring prosperity, ok?)

Crazy left thinks Islam is no more violent than Christians. This is what we've endured from lib-fictions.

The crazy left thinks Islam is no more violent than Christians: Lies we've endured for generations!

Any "rape culture" in California is from Jihadis or Professors, betcha

Won't give up their goal of globalist socialist internationalism while keeping America from defending herself.

I can't believe what idiots they've become. They're goaded to love awful things but hate the good--how dumb.

By resisting evil our spirits become stronger. This "animating contest" of liberty makes you younger.

I know how much it hurts to see your country get worse (as they lose their shirts)--pray and evil will disperse.

WALK TALL WITHIN WALLS

I know how much it hurts as evil gets the upper hand but by taking a stand God will take strong command!

We are shocked, in turmoil, sickened--but what can we do but turn to He who has always been true?

Getting ready for church (mod): Put on your armor against all things standing against God.

PANACEA: DELETE ALL RAINBOW FRIENDS

Panacea for all your ills: delete your rainbow friends. These are the weak who go along with trends.

Is it any wonder men have gotten sick of you broads? Button up and get some class--you look so odd!

If you condone something it's just like you doing it. Get that through your head sinner, stop confirming it.

Everyone's gone mad. They act tough but it's just a fad--the opposite to the era of mom and dad.

Who wants to spend time with a bunch of untrained, lewd children? Few mature, that is my wisdom.

They want you to suddenly become a dummy and agree with everything they say, or they betray.

There is beauty and wisdom in traditional marriage and parenting. The anti-family fems are unrelenting.

How dare you cross these lines, you communist leftist wicca feminists: Think of the kids, you amoralists.

HEALTHY UPDATES AND YOUTUBE MATES

If you're gonna eat inferior in your one meal a day you'll face stomach pains/detox the next day.

WALK TALL WITHIN WALLS

They fear sugar not their fatty desserts. Chocolate, coconut, nuts, nutbutters = GLYCATION.

I tried the rice noodles corn bread potatoes but even that was too much. Smoothis, soups and dips.

Office hours: These are the times I am not interrupted for any reason and to bother me is high treason!

Tedious details about non-issues to fill up time in order to maintain the channel and not be banned.

Due to your fear of losing your channel you've become guarded and boring-- what a shame darling.

After intense following of politics for 12 years I've now unsubbed from all news and discussions sir.

Us losing the election was a revolution. There's gonna be changes reverberating throughout the nation.

Most drive-by shooters are black so laws are seen as racist but black victims are hurt in the process.

I'm done with your boring fireside chats which are really just dribble from the rabble and very flat.

100 KAREN KELLOCK BOOKS

AFFINITY OR MISERY
AGELESS CORNUCOPIA
AMERICA AWAKE!
AMERICA'S DAFT ERA
ARTS OF PALEO FASTING
AUTOPHAGY ON CHEATERS
BACKSTABBING NEUROTICS
BETRAYAL TRAUMA
BOOMERS AND BROKENNESS
BOOT ON NECK
CHAMPION GUIDES
COMMIE NUTHOUSE
COMMIES
COMMUNIST SPIRIT
CONTAGION OF MADNESS
CONTAGIOUS MADNESS
CULTURE CLASH BASHED
DAFT LEFT
DAILY FASTARIAN
DAM RATS
DIVERSITY IS CRUELTY
E-RACE WHITE
EVIL FREAKS (Beyond Gross)
THE END OR A BEND?
FEMALE BULLIES AND FEMI-NAZIS
FEMALE CARNALITY
FEMALE DUMB DOWN
FEMALE POWER DRIVE
FEMINISM AND RUIN 1 & 2
FIX FOR MISFITS
FOOLS & TRAMPS
FREEDOM SPEAKING
FRENEMY ENABLER
FRENEMY LIAR
FRENEMY THIEF
FRENEMY TRAITOR
TRENEMY TYRANT
GENIUS IS HELD DOWN
GLOBALISLAM
GOD USES THE FLAWED
HAZE OF THE LATTER DAYS

THE HERD IN WORDS
HIX POLITIX
HOW THEY RUINED US
JUST SKIP DINNER
LE FEMME AND THE COMMUNIST SPIRIT
LIBERAL CHAOS & ROT
LIBERAL DOUBLETHINK
LIBERAL GALL 1 & 2
LIBERAL SHOVE-DOWNS
LOCK YOUR GATE
LOSERS and Femme Fatales
MANUAL FOR SUPERIOR MEN
MODERN ART FROM HELL
MOSTLY FAKE
NOTES TO CHAMPS 1 & 2
OVERCOME FRENEMIES
PC MAKES US CRAZY
PEOPLE ARE CRUEL
PEOPLE PROBLEMS 1 & 2
PERSECUTED GENIUIS
POLI-PSYCH MYSTERIES
PRETENTIOUS SLOBS
QUEEN BEE
RED NEW DEAL
RETURNING TO FIRST NATURE
SEASON OF TREASON
SEPARATE MEANS HOLY
SOCIAL HYPNOTISM
SOLITUDE SOLUTION
SUPERCILIOUS
THE SCHOOLS SCREWED EM UP
TOAD TO PRINCE
TRIALS CYCLES
TRUMP VS. GROUP
TRUST IN TRASH
THE TRUTH ABOUT PEOPLE
UNDERHEANDEDLY CLEVER
WALK TALL WITHIN WALLS
WE'RE NOT ALL ONE
WINNERS SKIP DINNER
WORK OR SMERK

KAREN KELLOCK PH.D.

M.S. Political Science, San Diego State. Ph.D. in Psychology, University of California Irvine. Postdoctoral: UCI School of Medicine, Dept. of Psychiatry [NIMH Grants]. Developed the Debris Theory of Disease, a theory of system pathology in 120 books and 22 textbooks for the general public. The theory has a general formula: All disease is obstruction, all recovery is elimination, all success is attraction. The three obstructions are people, habit and food. Remove obstruction and snap to your goals, waiting in the wings.